Telepathy for Beginners

Experiments, Instructions, Examples and Models

Contact: www.HarryEilenstein.de
Harry.Eilenstein@web.de
Harry Eilenstein at youtube

Imprint: Copyright: 2011 by Harry Eilenstein – All rights reserved, including but not limited to that of translation. No part of this book may be reproduced, translated, stored in a retrieval system, or transmitted in any form or by any means, electronic, mechanical, photocopying, recording, or otherwise, without the prior written permission of the author and the publisher.

Production and publishing house: BoD – Books on Demand, Norderstedt

ISBN: 9783741282157

Table of Contents

1. Characteristics of Telepathy — 4
   *a) Telepathy in everyday life   b) Examples in religion and magic
   c) Examples of my own experience   d) Summary*
2. The Development of a Telepathy Model — 13
   *a) The procedure of a chemist   b) The "classical" telepathy experiment
   c) The Pendulum   d) The "Zombie Experiment"   e) The Postcard Experiment
   f) Summary*
3. Experiments with the Telepathy Model — 22
   a) Dream journeys   b) Collective telepathy   c) Hypnosis   d) Summary
4. Border Areas of Telepathy — 28
   *a) Wishes   b) Omens and oracles   c) Telekinesis   d) Astral projection
   e) Magic   f) Poltergeists   g) Homeopathy   h) Materializations
   i) The ABC of the Sorcerer's Apprentice   j) Summary*
5. The Content of the "Telepathic Transmission" — 42
6. Special Forms of Telepathy — 48
   *a) Automatic writing   b) The "cloak of invisibility"
   c) Transfer of consciousness   d) Time telepathy
   e) Sending and receiving   f) Sensitive computers   g) Summary*
7. Telepathy in the Horoscope — 52
8. Telepathy Models — 54
9. Telepathy in Everyday Life — 55
10. Learning Telepathy — 56

    Book List — 58

1. Characteristics of Telepathy

1. a) Telepathy in everyday life

Who has not experienced this – one walks through the city and suddenly has a strange feeling and turns around and sees that from behind an acquaintance comes hurrying up, who has just recognized one. You felt something and reacted to it without knowing exactly what was going on.

Until 10,000 years ago, before the development of agriculture and animal husbandry in the early Neolithic period, this "funny feeling" was a vital skill: If a hungry tiger was lurking behind some bushes, it was decidedly helpful if you could sense its hungry gaze …

Telepathy is an essential element in almost all religious, mythological, spiritual, esoteric and magical world views – even if it is not always called "telepathy".

This widespread use is not surprising, because telepathy is ultimately an "inner connection" between two beings – and religion and magic are ultimately about such "inner connections" all the time.

Even the word "religion" means "re-connection", that is, "backing up to the gods". This can be interpreted, if one wants to do so, also as "telepathic connection to the gods" – whereby "telepathy" would already have a very broad meaning in this context. But religion is essentially already the invisible, non-physical connection of humans to their ancestors, to the gods or to God.

Telepathy seems to be an important topic …

1. b) Examples from religion and magic

In the New Testament, an example of advanced telepathy is found in Matthew 17:24-27:

Now when they came to Capernaum, those who were collecting the two-drachma tax ("temple tax") *came to Peter and said, "Does not your master pay the tax?"*
He said, "Yes."
And when he came into the house, Jesus preceded him (Jesus telepathically

discerned what Peter had experienced.) *and said, "What do you mean, Simon? From whom do the kings of the earth take tolls or taxes: from their sons or from strangers?"*

Then Peter said to him, "From strangers."

Jesus said to him, "So the sons are free. But lest we give them offence, go to the sea, and cast a line, and the first fish that comes up, take him; and when you open his mouth, you will find a two-drachma piece; take that, and give it to them for me and for you." (Jesus telepathically recognized these circumstances in the future.)

- - -

In the Old Testament, Elijah and his disciple Elisha are especially known for their magical abilities. Thus it is said of Elisha in the 2nd Book of Kings 6:27-32:

> *When the king heard the woman's words, he tore his clothes as he walked on the wall. Then all the people saw that he had the sackcloth on his body underneath.*
>
> *And he said, "God do this to me and that, if Elisha son of Shaphat keeps his head today!"* (Death sentence for Elisha)
>
> *And Elisha sat in his house, and the elders sat with him. And the king sent a man before him.*
>
> *But before the messenger came to him, Elisha said to the elders, "Have you seen how he* (the king) *has sent this murderer here to cut off my head?"*

- - -

In Tibetan Buddhism, telepathy is also reported quite frequently – especially in connection with meditations on deceased yogis, but also in everyday events.

For example, after an argument with the monk Dharlo, the Tibetan yogi Milarepa finally told Dharlo that Dharlo had given two necklaces from the monastery property to a woman so that she would become his mistress – this was telepathically perceived by Milarepa.

- - -

The monk Lotön tested Milarepa the next day by performing a ritual wrongly in his chamber – whereupon Milarepa greeted him the next day with the words that Lotön should refrain from such mischief in the future.

- - -

One can also find telepathy apart from the "great religions" – e.g. with the shaman and war chief Geronimo from the tribe of the Apaches:

Geronimo, as a shaman, also learned astral journey and used it extensively to fly regularly in his astral body to the camps of the cavalry to spy on what they had planned next. In this way, he was able to resist the militarily far superior cavalry for 35 years.

- - -

There are also reports of telepathy in the Germanic tradition – for example, in the "Book of Land-taking", which tells of the settlement of Iceland:

> *Heid the Spellsong Woman* (seer) *predicted to them all that they would settle in a land to the west of the sea* (Iceland) *that had not yet been discovered, but Ingimund said that he would beware of it. The magic song woman, however, said that he would not be able to do that and that, as a sign of that, his talisman, which he carried in his pocket, would now disappear and that he would find it again where he was digging on that land for the foundation for the pillar behind his high seat.*
>
> *... ... ...*
>
> *Ingimund did not feel at home anywhere; so King Harald urged him to seek his fortune in Iceland. Ingimund said that this was what he had never intended to do, but he sent two Finns as Hamfarir* (shapeshifters) *on a mage's journey* (astral journey) *to Iceland to look for his talisman, which was shaped in the form of Freyr and made of silver.*
>
> *The Finns came back and said that they had found the place where the talisman was, but that they could not seize it.*
>
> *However, they described to Ingimund exactly the location of the place in a valley between two hills, and they told Ingimund all the details of the land and how it was shaped, where he was to settle.*
>
> *After that Ingimund left for his journey to Iceland. With him went his brother-in-law Jorund Nacken and his friends Eyvindr Sorkvir and Asmund and Hvyti and his servants Fridmund, Bodvar, Thorir, Refskegg and Ulfkell.*
>
> *They came ashore in the southern part of Iceland and stayed in Hvanneyri all winter, together with Grim, Ingimund's foster-brother, but in the spring they went north over the heath.*
>
> *Then they came to an arm of the sea where they found two rams and called it Rams' Bay. From there they continued to wander northward across the land, giving appropriate names to all the places they came to.*
>
> *He stayed for one winter in Vidi Valley in Ingimunds Forest. From there they saw snowless mountains to the south and moved south there. There Ingimund recognized the appearance of the land that the seer had described as his future home.*

Thordis, his daughter, was born in Thordis Forest.
Ingimund took possession of the whole water-valley from Helga-water and Urdar-water upwards and lived in Hof and found his talisman there at the place where he dug the foundation for his high-post.

1. c)   **Examples from my own experience**

I also include here some of my own experiences, as I can describe them most accurately – which is helpful for the study of telepathy.

- - -

When I was 20 years old I met Annette. She told me after a few days about a vacation in the south of France. Suddenly I saw the landscape she had been in front of me and could continue telling what she had experienced. Something like that became normal between us pretty soon.

We always knew for sure whether the other one was at home or where he/she was in the city or in the forest.

- - -

Once when Annette was visiting me, she suddenly thoughtfully said that all kinds of colors were shining in my room. When I asked her what she saw, she began to describe it to me in great detail.

She saw exactly what I imagined every day in my room. At that time I was accepted by a magician as a sorcerer's apprentice and thereupon I first learned how to draw a protective circle. For this I used the "Lesser Pentagram Ritual" and the "Exercise of the Middle Pillar".

Annette described to me the white radiant circle on the floor, the four flaming pentagrams on the four walls, the golden hexagram on the ceiling, the four archangels in the four directions and the Middle Pillar consisting of five colored spheres in the center of the room.

- - -

A few months later, one of my sisters, who lived in the room next to me, came to me in the morning and said that she had had a very strange dream. When I asked her, she told me that she had seen me standing in my room, making gestures, speaking softly, and how a colorful picture had appeared in my room.

She also described to me the pentagram ritual and the Middle Pillar with many details.

- - -

My grandparents tried several times to surprise my mother by coming unannounced from Hamburg to visit us in Bonn. But the surprise never worked, because my mother always sensed that and therefore cooked more and baked a cake.

- - -

My grandfather (my mother's father) had once had knee pain for a long time and no doctor could help him. Then a neighbor advised him to go to a healer who lived a few villages away. When he opened the door of the healer's house, he saw that she was plucking a chicken. Then the feathers of the chicken all flew to my grandfather and stuck to him.

Then the healer said to my grandfather that he obviously had much greater powers than she did and that she therefore unfortunately could not help him …

- - -

My great-grandmother (my grandfather's mother) also had this talent: she sometimes went to the fair with us children and our grandparents and parents. Once, when I drew only blanks, she told me that this would not do and that she would buy me a ticket now. My parents tried to explain to her how the lottery works and that there are a lot of blanks. However, she bought a single ticket without further ado and drew the main prize.

A few years later, one of my sisters had bad luck with the tickets and my great-grandmother also drew the main prize for her with a single ticket.

I don't think she was very popular with the fair people ….

They say in Holstein that this talent is passed on from father to daughter and from mother to son – at least with my great-grandmother, my grandfather, my mother and me this is true. After that, however, it goes on to my son – but he was not born in Holstein …

- - -

When I was accepted as a magician's apprentice by a magician at the age of 21, we experimented quite wildly. Since he had a German shepherd dog, we wondered if dogs could also perceive telepathically. So we both imagined a white rabbit in front of his nose.

The effect was quite interesting – imitation recommended.

- - -

When I was about 24 years old I went to a friend with whom I learned goldsmithing. I made a piece of jewelry for my friend Jörg. When I was finished, I had the strange feeling that I should take it to his apartment in Bonn right away – although we had arranged to meet the next day. So I drove to his place – this is extremely untypical behavior for me, since I always try to keep all appointments as precisely as possible.

When I then stood in front of his door and he opened it for me, he looked surprised and then had to laugh quite a bit – he had called me by telephone, but had not reached me anywhere and therefore sat down and inwardly called me to him, because he urgently needed the piece of jewelry a day earlier.

Apparently, his "call" reached me and was also so loud that it drowned out all my concerns about the arranged appointment …

In retrospect, it was amusing to see how many arguments I came up with on the way to be able to go to Jörg's a day earlier, despite my principle of sticking as closely as possible to agreements.

- - -

Once I went with my bicycle to Frater U.D. in the Siebengebirge (where he lived at that time), where we wanted to do some experiments with several people. Thereby a screw at the axle of my bicycle had loosened. When I asked him for a 12mm wrench, he said he had just moved in and had no idea where anything was.

Since the group that met there had met their power animals shortly before, I inwardly asked my she-wolf where there was a 12-key. Thereupon she showed me a drawer in a cupboard in the living room – there I found the 12-key.

- - -

When my son was born (he came three months early) and I gently reached out to him with my index finger, he opened his eyes and inwardly said very clearly, "Hello, I'm David." I was completely taken aback, as I had never heard of such a thing.

However, as I have since learned, it seems to happen quite often that newborns tell their parents their names.

After that, David kept his eyes closed for a few months – as is usual with premature babies.

I then called a friend because he had come into the world with a cesarean section and a lot of chaos. The friend in turn called Mary Bauermeister and asked her for help for mother and child. They looked inwardly at who had come into the world and gave him a name ("Papageno") that fit his character and sent him protection inwardly. Later they described to me the character they had seen – the later development showed that they had judged him exactly right.

- - -

My former wife lost a daughter about six months old in a miscarriage. A few hours later I sat down at the sea and went inwardly to our dead daughter Miriam to accompany her soul to the otherworld. I saw her soul immediately … but I didn't need to accompany her because she knew the way much better than I did – instead she told and showed me some things.

I wanted to help her and instead I received a gift from her …

- - -

Then, a few years later, when my daughter Susanna was born, I turned inwardly to her soul and asked her what she wanted to be called in this life. I saw her soul immediately and she also told me her name.

- - -

When David was between 6 and 10 years old, we often played various guessing games. At some point he noticed that I could "read" the answers in his head. This resulted in a new game variant: He asked a question and then concentrated on a wrong answer – for example, I answered the question "What is the capital of Australia?" with "Sydney", although I know exactly that it is Canberra and not Sydney. He had concentreted on "Sydney", of course …

He really enjoyed this variation of the game.

- - -

When my son and I are together and I think something that relates to him, or consider asking him something or suggesting something to him, he asks every time before I've opened my mouth, "What did you say?" I can count on that question.

- - -

With both my son and my daughter, I have also experienced it many times that I wanted to ask them something and they came up with the answer before I could ask the question. Sometimes they were convinced that I really asked aloud.

- - -

I once met a woman at a seminar. We were immediately sympathetic to each other. In the evening, when we were all sitting together at dinner, I went to the food counter to get seconds. There I heard the woman inwardly rather loudly say that she would like an apple. So I looked at her a bit surprised, took an apple and threw it to her.

Just because of her astonished face this experience was worthwhile, because she had actually just thought that she would like to have still another apple and that I should bring one.

- - -

A few years ago I had read something about Leonardo da Vinci and once again marveled at all his observations and inventions. Thereupon I asked David whether he knows why one day after new moon one can see not only the thin moon crescent, but dimly the whole moon.

He immediately answered, "It's because of the sunlight reflecting off the earth and hitting the moon." He answered spontaneously, never having thought about the subject before – and simply tapped into my knowledge of Leonardo's discovery. Very handy for exams …

- - -

David was once driving to a birth celebration with some friends when they missed a bus a few miles from their destination. That's when David said that the house they were going to must be about on the other side of the woods from where he was standing with his friends.

So he let his inner voice guide him through the nighttime forest he didn't know, and he and his friends came out right at the garden gate behind the house they were going to.

- - -

There is a simple game to practice telepathy: When you need the time, you can look inside where the next church tower or similar is and try to read the time there – and then check the telepathically seen time on your own watch or on your own cell phone.

- - -

In the course of time I have experienced very many things like this and also heard like things from others, but I don't tell them all now, because this book would become rather heyvy and this chapter is only about describing the different ways in which telepathy can occur or in which I have experienced telepathy so far.

1. d) Summary

From the examples given, one can already see some peculiarities of telepathy:

One can perceive things telepathically both consciously, purposefully and with intention, and unconsciously and, so to speak, incidentally.

Telepathically perceived things can also appear as dreams. So the waking consciousness is not necessary for telepathy itself.

Not only single informations or motives can be perceived, but also complex pictures (pentagram ritual, vacation landscape).

One can consciously send out a thought and summon someone.

Several people can perceive something together (e.g. the women who helped my just born son and saw his character in this context).

There are "helpers" in telepathy such as the power animals.

Telepathy can also be used systematically and with great reliability in life-threatening situations (Geronimo in the war with the cavalry). Telepathy, therefore, with proper practice, need not be a vague matter of hunches and guesses.

It would seem that telepathy is one phenomenon out of a broader group of phenomena (the feathers flying at my grandfather and the like).

The examplesthat have been told here are of course no proof of telepathy – except of course for myself, because I have experienced these things.

Therefore, in the next chapter follow some examples of experiments that you can do yourself and with which you can easily and reliably experience telepathy yourself.

2. The Development of a Telepathy Model

If you want to ride a bicycle, it is helpful if you understand at least roughly how a bicycle works, what function the individual components have and, if possible, how you can repair a bicycle.

Therefore, in this chapter follows the attempt to design a model of telepathy that is as accurate as possible, i.e. to find a description of telepathy that is a good fundament for one's strategy in telepathy experiments and in telepathy applications.

This description will then make it possible to see what one must do to obtain a desired telepathic effect when one needs it.

2. a) The procedure of a chemist

How can one recognize a thing as precisely as possible?

First of all, it is helpful if one knows what one actually wants to recognize – and preferably also why. Curiosity and thirst for knowledge is a sufficient and solid motivation …

To be able to recognize something, you have to observe it, you have to experience it. Without one's own experience there is nothing to think about …

Either, therefore, you simply look at what you happen to have experienced, or you think of experiments that you can perform to see how a thing behaves.

An experiment has a number of different phases, which can be readily observed in a chemist, for example.

> The first phase of an experiment is to clarify the aforementioned motivation to better understand, and therefore better use, something specific.
>
> The second phase is the observation of what is already known and of what one knows to be true or that it could possibly be true. For example, the chemist wants to better understand a particular chemical compound and its variations and possible applications.
>
> The third phase is the design of an experiment, by which one will possibly experience something, which one did not know before or what he does not know precisely – finally it concerns to recognize something new and for it

one needs new experiences. The chemist therefore considers, for example, which chemical he could tip into the chemical compound he wants to understand better.

In the fourth phase, the chemist checks which precautionary measures are useful: protective goggles, gloves, extinguisher nearby ... For new telepathy experiments, for example, it might be useful not to do them while driving a car, but first at home in a protected setting. It is also best not to make such a telepathy attempt when a lot depends on the result – unless you have no other choice anyway ...

In the fifth phase the experiment is carried out. The chemist observes as closely as possible and notes down what is perceived. It is important to observe only, not to ignore or emphasize anything, but to be neutral like a white sheet of paper or like a photograph. In other words, not rejecting anything, criticizing or saying "That can't be!".

The sixth phase consists of arranging and interpreting all observations. This may lead to new ideas about what could have happened during the experiment and which model best describes the observed process.

Finally, in the seventh phase, new questions arise from this, which again lead to new experiments.

This procedure brings also into parapsychology, into religion, into esotericism and into magic a down-to-earth objectivity, which generally has a quite beneficial effect.

2. b) The "classical" telepathy experiment

The best known telepathy experiment, used mainly in parapsychology, consists of one person guessing the cards another one is looking at.
For this, 25 cards are used, on which there are 5 different symbols – each symbol is represented five times.
From the frequency with which the cards are correctly "guessed", the probability can be calculated precisely, with which the result is not coincidence, but telepathy.

This experimental setup assumes that telepathy is something like seeing with the eyes. Probably largely unspoken, this experiment is also based on the assumption that telepathy can be controlled at will by the waking consciousness – just as one can look at the place one just decides to look at.

For this experimental arrangement speaks that its results are easily verifiable and the telepathy probability can be calculated exactly. With this experiment results have occurred again and again, which are clearly outside the normal probabilities.

Against this experimental arrangement speaks that telepathy can take place also unconsciously, as a sideline or even in a dream. This shows clearly that telepathy cannot be compared to the normal seeing with the eyes, which is coupled to the waking consciousness.

Further it speaks against this experimental arrangement that a clear fatigue symptom could be observed with it: the first few attempts, which a person accomplished, were almost always more successful than the later attempts. This also shows that telepathy cannot be compared to the seeing with the eyes, because with normal seeing the recognition of what one sees in front of oneself becomes better with increasing practice first for a longer time – until finally sometime much later a general fatigue and lack of concentration occurs.

So it makes sense to change the telepathy experiments and to adapt them to these findings.

2. c) __The pendulum__

There is an experiment that can be used to get closer to the processes that take place in a person during telepathy.

In normal vision, a ray of light arrives in the eye, stimulates a receptor inside the back of the eyeball, which transmits this impulse to the brain, where the totality of impulses from the two optic nerves leading from the eyes to the brain is processed, i.e. the structure of what is seen is analyzed and compared with already stored structures. Finally, for example, the realization arises that one sees an apple in front of oneself.

It would be interesting to know what is going on during telepathy and where these processes take place.
First of all it is only known that at the end of the process a conscious or semi-conscious cognition arises in the brain – the telepathic perception.
Besides it is still known that there is no physical sense organ like the eye which perceives the telepathically received information.
Finally, the third thing that is known is that telepathy is not only receiving, but also sending. Telepathy is, so to speak, hearing ear and calling mouth at the same time.

A pendulum is a very simple telepathy tool. It consists of a small object on a string. This need not be a gold-set diamond on a silk cord – for years I just hung my front door key on my headband when I needed a pendulum.

When you use the pendulum, you hold it in your hand on your bent (rather than propped up) arm in front of you. As a rule, it hangs there relatively quietly and only wobbles back and forth a little uncoordinatedly.

However, you can ask the pendulum a question such as "Am I hungry?" and then see what it does in response.

Broadly speaking, the pendulum has five possible movements: back and forth; from left to right and back again; clockwise in a circle; counterclockwise in a circle; and finally just hanging there motionless.

You can now tell the pendulum that, for example, "back and forth" should mean "yes" and "sideways" should mean "no". Whether this arrangement with the pendulum works can be easily checked by asking a few questions: "Am I a man?", "Is it daytime?", "Am I on earth?" etc. For example, for "turn counterclockwise" you can set the meaning "please formulate the question differently" and for "turn clockwise" you can set the meaning "nonsensical question".

When the pendulum has been programmed in this way, so to speak, you can now do some experiments.

One person hides a key in the apartment and a second person tries to find this key with the help of the pendulum's answers to his own questions: "Is the key in front of me?", "Is the key above my waistline?", "Is the key in this room?", and so on. The pendulum can answer "yes" and "no" to these questions. Then you follow the answers of the pendulum in order to find the key.

You can also do the same experiment by having a third person hide the key beforehand. By doing this, you rule out the possibility, since you get the information from a person present who knows where the key is.

Finally, one can also ask a person to think of something and then try to find out what they are thinking of with the help of the pendulum-answers to your questions about this topic.

One can think about what is actually going on after these experiments. In doing so, one should adhere to the scientific principle that the theory with the fewest additional assumptions is probably the correct one. Or in other words: Correct models are mostly simple and elegant.

The pendulum itself is quite certainly not what performs telepathy – otherwise you would always need a pendulum for telepathy. However, the pendulum is what makes the telepathically obtained information visible. So the pendulum is a monitor. But for what is the pendulum the monitor?

At least the "cable on the monitor" can be recognized: these are the muscles of the arm, whose tiny but coordinated movements cause the swinging of the pendulum.

One can trace this process one step further back: The tiny but coordinated movements of the arm are controlled by the nerves that lead from the brain to the arm muscles.

One can even go one more step further towards the origin of the information: One is not aware of the answers of the pendulum, but only sees them by means of the pendulum. The telepathically obtained information is therefore first in the subconsciousness before it reaches the consciousness via the pendulum. So the pendulum is a monitor for the subconsciousness.

This is basically the same as with the feeling that you are being stared at from behind: You spontaneously (i.e. subconsciously) turn around because something feels "funny."

If you do these pendulum experiments for a longer time, you will eventually be able to feel what the pendulum is about to do – the waking consciousness has become a second monitor for telepathy besides the pendulum …

2. d) The "zombie experiment"

The pendulum is very practical and you can use it in all kinds of situations. Of course, one should not just blindly follow the statements of the pendulum, but simply see its answers as information, the origin of which one does not know exactly, and look in what way the answers may help oneself.

However, there are situations where getting a pendulum out could lead to complications – for example, at conferences. When I was confronted with this problem, I thought about what I could do. The solution was quite simple.

If it is the muscles of the arm that make the pendulum swing, then one would have to be able to "program" other muscles as well. So I put my right hand over my left forearm in such a way that all the fingers were hanging relaxed in the air. Then I asked the fingers of my right hand which of them wanted to stand for "yes". Thereupon my index finger moved slightly. The middle finger took the "no", the ring finger the "imprecise question" and the little finger the "nonsensical question!".

After that, when I once wanted to elicit some information in a conference, all I had to do was put my right hand over my left forearm, inwardly ask my question, and then see which finger moved slightly in response.

Problem solved.

Soon after, I tried to see if it wasn't also possible to tell my arm to move. The experience was quite funny: I told my right arm to move and saw what happened. It did indeed rise, but I was only the spectator at my own arm movement and no longer the one moving my arm.

When I showed this experiment to my friend Jörg, we started to try it with two arms at the same time, with the legs and so on. Finally I told my body "get up and go to Jörg and touch him".

Then I witnessed how my own body moved, stood up and walked and then touched Jörg's arm with one hand. Jörg also clearly felt that this was something completely different than an arbitrary, deliberate movement. The movement made him shiver and he commented, "Only zombies are better!" That's where this experiment got its name.

Many years later, I asked myself what useful things could be done with this zombie experiment. Then I thought that the whole body is controlled from the subconsciousness similar to a sleepwalker and that the telepathic information is first of all in the subconsciousness before it comes into the waking consciousness. Could one therefore tell one's own body to obtain information telepathically and then subsequently perform an action corresponding to that information?

The next time my son visited me, I explained to him what I wanted to experiment. I had previously hidden a key in my apartment under the edge of a carpet for this purpose. David practiced a bit until he could tell his body to move on its own.

I then told him that I had hidden a key in my apartment. He told his body to get the key and saw what his body did. Standing up in this state is always a jerky buckling in the hip that looks like the person is about to fall over. David strode purposefully through the apartment with these strange "zombie steps," stopped at the edge of the carpet, and then buckled forward at the hip, his arm dropping down under the carpet as if with a kind of pendulum motion, and pulled out the key without David seeing it first.

So the attempt was a complete success.

A few months later David had big problems with his hamstrings and he was to have surgery at both knees. When he was on a class trip to Nuremberg and was standing with his crutches on top of the courtyard of the castle, he thought that it must be possible to heal the knees with magic. So he told his body to lead him to his healing. Thereupon he walked purpose-fully on his crutches towards a small gate, the door of which was unexpectedly unlocked.

He came to a small herb garden. Purposefully his body led him to a certain bed, where his upper body bent forward again, his hand falling forward (the same kind of fluid movement as with the search for the key), tore off some leaves of a plant and with the same fluid movement put them into his mouth. After eating these leaves, he was able to tuck his crutches under his arm and he was completly healthy again.

So telepathy works not only between two people, and not only between a person and an object (12-key for my bicycle) – apparently you can also telepathically obtain information that leads to a cure, even though no one knew how to cure your knees before.

So it looks like telepathy can be not only a "line" between two people or a "line" between a person and an object, but that a single telepathic perception is a part of a large "network of lines" in which there is information that one did not know about.

So telepathy seems to be something like the flow of information on the internet.

Some years later David became a Parcour trainer and Ninja warrior. He uses this telepathic and telekinetic methods also to help his pupils learn the jumps, rolls, climbings and so on and to heal smaller wounds and pains or to overcome inner and outer obstacles.

It's a bit like an apprenticeship with Master Yoda…

2. e) <u>The postcard experiment</u>

The previous considerations now make it possible to design a new telepathy experiment.

If the telepathic information first arrives in the subconsciousness and then has to be fetched from there into the waking consciousness, there is the problem that one does not know what belongs to the telepathic information and what is simply an association.

So one receives a message that is accompanied by noise. So the question is how to construct a filter that can separate the telepathic information from the noise. Fortunately, the solution for this problem is quite simple.

Ideally, a whole school class or a similarly large group participates in the experiment. For the experiment one needs further about twenty as different as possible postcards (or photos) with striking motives. These postcards are put into envelopes, which are sealed so that the postcards are no longer visible.

Now the class is divided into groups of four. Each group sits at a table and receives an envelope that is placed in the middle of the table. Now everyone concentrates for about three minutes on the postcard in the envelope and then writes down all impressions on a piece of paper – this writing down is necessary so that no one adds anything to their perceptions or leaves anything out afterwards.

Then the perceptions are compared. The things that all four or at least three of the four students have perceived are obviously telepathic perceptions, because it is extremely unlikely that four people have the same imagination.

If they now perceived e.g. "a lot of blue", "warmth", "noise" and a "yellow spot", this sounds very much like a beach scene with sun.

Now you can fill in this framework with the things that two of the four students saw. For example, if one student saw a tree and one student saw a palm tree, there will probably still be a palm tree on the beach picture.

The perceptions that are only associations, i.e. "noise", are different for each of the four students and fall out of the description of the telepathically seen picture in this procedure.

One can, of course, just do this experiment with four persons, but if six groups or more correctly recognize their image at the same time, it has a much greater persuasive power …

2. f) Summary

The experiments so far now already allow the formulation of a somewhat more sophisticated telepathy model.

On the basis of the experiments and experiences described so far, the following characteristics of telepathy can be identified:

> Telepathy connects people with people, people with things, and people with an as yet unexplained source of information that knows, for example, the way to a spontaneous healing.
>
> Telepathically perceived things can also appear as dreams. So the waking consciousness is not necessary for telepathy itself.
>
> The telepathic information first reaches the subconsciousness, which also processes it, as e.g. looking around when being stared at from behind shows.
>
> One can perceive things telepathically consciously, purposefully and with intention, but also unconsciously and so to speak incidentally.
>
> In order to become conscious, the telepathically acquired information must reach the waking consciousness. This can happen by a dream, by a monitor like the pendulum, a muscle movement like in the "finger programming" or in the "zombie experiment" or by a direct awareness.
>
> Not only single informations or motives can be perceived, but also complex pictures (pentagram ritual, vacation landscape).
>
> One can consciously send out a thought and summon someone.

No minimum age is necessary for telepathy, as my experiences with my son show, which started immediately after his birth ("Hello, I am David.").

Also wrong information can be sent telepathically to the consciousness – and the knowledge of another person can be disturbed telepathically so effectively that this other person unintentionally says wrong things ("Sydney instead of Canberra as the capital of Australia").

Several people can perceive something together (postcard experiment).

There are "helpers" in telepathy such as the power animals.

Telepathy can also be used systematically and with great reliability in life-threatening situations (Geronimo in the war with the cavalry). Telepathy, therefore, with proper practice, need not be a vague matter of hunches and guesses.

It would seem that telepathy is one phenomenon from a broader group of phenomena that includes telekinesis (the feathers flying at my grandfather and the like).

From this informations results as a model a general information abundance, which consists among other things of a large quantity of telepathic connections. The contact to this abundance of information lies in the subconsciousness.

The human being has the ability to send telepathically (Sydney instead of Canberra) as well as to receive intentionally (postcard experiment) and to receive unintentionally (being stared at).

The telepathically attainable wealth of information seems to be more than just information, as it also contains telekinetic phenomena. This means that telepathic sending could be a special case of telekinesis: A "magical" effect emanates from a human being.

3. Experiments with the Telepathy Model

In order to find out more exactly what telepathy is and how it works, further new experiments are now necessary.

3. a) Dream journeys

A dream journey consists in the conscious coordination of waking consciousness and subconsciousness – this sounds complicated, but is simple.

If you wake up from a dream in the morning and consciously continue dreaming it for another 10 seconds, during which it still keeps its momentum, you are in this dream journey state.

If, for example, you look out of the window in the train and get into a longer daydream and then suddenly wake up and realize that you are not on the beach on your last vacation at all, but sitting in the train, you have also been in this state.

You can also consciously evoke this state. To do this, you lie down relaxed and concentrate on a topic that you have chosen beforehand. One can either simply decide on the theme for the upcoming dream journey completely informally, one can step in one's imagination through a symbol that stands for the selected theme, or one can inwardly address a deity, an animal, a plant or another being and start a conversation with it.

In the beginning, you have to get used to accepting all impressions first and taking them seriously, but this actually happens quite quickly.

Dream journeys are easiest to learn by doing them a few times together with someone who already has some practice in it.

With these dream journeys you don't need a monitor anymore, because you yourself go fully conscious to the level of the subconsciousness. Or formulated differently: One consciously opens the waking consciousness to all the information that belongs to a certain subject, so that it can enter the waking consciousness from the subconsciousness.

This entering into dream journey imagery is much like typing a search term into an Internet browser, which then searches for everything there is to that term.

One can use dream journeys to explore one's own inner self, but with dream journeys one can also access information that is only been accessible telepathically.

One can also visit plants in this way and learn from them their healing effects – thus telepathy between man and plant. The same works with stones (crystal healing), planets (astrology) and all other things on earth.

In this way, one can also look at other places in a very concrete way and see what it looks like there. One can then check these perceptions afterwards by physically going to these places and checking one's own perceptions.

When I once told a friend about this on the phone, she immediately asked me "What color are the underpants I'm wearing right now?" In response, I checked internally and told her accurately, which left her quite stunned.

You may also look into the inside of other persons to help them understand their psychic problems or their health problems.

3. b)   Collective telepathy

So far, only forms of telepathy have been described in which a human being and another human being, animal or plant were involved, or in which the telepathically acquired information came from a realm which at first could not be more closely grasped.

There is a whole series of phenomena which show that telepathy can also be a group process or a collective phenomenon.

I have often undertaken dream journeys in pairs on a subject that interested both of us. In almost every dream journey the effect occurred several times that I saw something and that the other person started to describe it before I had said anything about it. The same thing happened in reverse.

The perceptions involved were often not just simple things like "I see a tree." but more exotic things like "Hmm, I see a dragon – and it has a bandage on its left front paw."

These experiences clearly show that both dream travelers are actually in the same vision.

In such dream journeys, one converses with each other while one is on the move – much like taking a hike through a valley and talking besides about the landscape.

Such joint dream journeys can also be undertaken by four or five people – with even more people it gradually becomes confusing. Also in these group dream trips, everyone is in the same picture and experiencing the same things.

Probably the best known form of group telepathy at the moment are the systemic family constellations. This involves a group of people meeting to seek healing. This works as follows:

The person seeking healing tells what situation they are in, and the leader of the constellation then decides which people are important in the healing seeker's story – for example, their parents, wife, and son. Then the other participants are asked who would like to represent these people.

These people then all place themselves in a designated area in the room (e.g. on a large carpet) and see what they intuitively want to do. It then very quickly becomes apparent that these "actors" are actually connected to the persons they represent, because although they know next to nothing about the persons they represent, but they speak like them, are choleric like them, and limp like them.

In the family constellation, the entire situation of the person seeking healing is, so to speak, telepathically summoned and intuitively enacted by the "actors".

Not only people, but also parts of the psyche of the person seeking advice, the planets from his horoscope, his hometown and everything else can be represented in this way by an "actor".

In the end, you have to have experienced such a constellation to be able to imagine what happens and how it feels – just like collective telepathy.

There are also "involuntary mini family constellations". This happens when you are with someone and you are drawn into a role that the other person has in them because of their past experiences. Then you start to behave differently than you normally would – but most of the time you only notice this if you are quite attentive to what you want, feel, think and do.

In spiritism, the spirits of the deceased are summoned and consulted using a method similar to scrying ("Quija board").

This is basically a procedure similar to family constellations. Such requests for advice and help to the ancestors exist in very many forms. The family constellations originate e.g. from South Africa from the medicine men there. Spiritism is a European variant. The Utiseta ritual of the Germanic tribes is a method that was widespread in northern and central Europe until the Middle Ages, when it was demonized by the church as "necromancy". The Celts also had such a ritual. Among the Chinese, it has been customary for a very long time to go to the ancestral shrine for advice and help.

In most religious or magical rituals, a form of collective telepathy also takes place – everyone is focused on the same words, images, symbols and processes, experiencing similar things. However, this usually only becomes apparent when performing somewhat more individualized rituals with a high enough intensity.

One can also count mass psychosis, mass panic and similar phenomena among the phenomena of collective telepathy. However, these phenomena are not suitable for proving telepathy per se, since they can also be explained without telepathy.

However, these phenomena become more understandable if telepathy has already been proved and therefore is added to the explanation: When a large enough number of people feel or imagine the same thing, a pull or current is created that draws almost all other people into these feelings and imaginings.

Finally, there is the "phenomenon of the hundredth monkey," which has been named after the event where this was first observed.

On an island near Japan, monkeys were fed potatoes. After a while, a monkey discovered that the potatoes were more pleasant to eat if he washed them in the stream beforehand. Little by little, some monkeys imitated him and removed the earth and sand from the potatoes in the water. This imitation effect was quite slow, but when a certain number of monkeys learned to wash the potatoes, all the monkeys did it at once – and all the monkeys on all the other islands, too, who had not known about this discovery on one of the islands.

This is so to say a peaceful variant of the dynamics with a mass panic – if a certain number of humans (or monkeys) wants, feels, thinks, sees or does the same, sudenly all at once do it.

This phenomenon confirms the suggestion that telepathy is not just individual "telepathic threads" between individual people, animals, plants and things, but that the individual telepathic event is part of a larger "organism" in which the individual telepathic event is a "cell", so to speak.

My son works at the GSI ("Gesellschaft für Schwerionenforschung" = "Helmholz Centre for Heavy Ion Research") in Darmstadt, Germany, developing image processing procedures for the various experiments that are conducted there. We talk from time to time about what he is doing there and what possible solutions he has discovered – even though I cannot follow him on the programming level, but only on the general level, since I myself have not learned programming.

A few weeks ago I woke up and already in my dream I started to think about a problem I had encountered in electronic image processing. I thought about this problem for about an hour and a half (which I usually never do) and then did something else.

Two days later I talked to David on the phone and told him about my thoughts and my ideas for a solution. He told me that he had also discovered this problem and had been thinking about it for a few days and that he had found the solution that very morning at the time when I was also thinking about it.

Did I simply hear telepathically quite precisely what David was thinking about, or did we couple our two consciousnesses to solve the problem together?

The group dream journeys show that there is such telepathic coordination of inner images – why not use it to solve problems?

Extended a little further, you have the "swarm consciousness" of some animal species … and with still a little more coordination, you get the collective subconsciousness …

3. c) Hypnosis

Another phenomenon that also has a telepathy side is hypnosis. The hypnotist speaks softly but firmly to the person to be hypnotized. He suggests to him that he relaxes, becomes tired, becomes heavy, becomes pleasantly warm, and finally falls asleep. In the process, the hypnotist gradually takes control of the other person.

The process is similar to a family constellation, where the performer allows himself to be guided telepathically by a certain person and embodies him (e.g., the father of the person seeking healing).

It is also the same process as a person unconsciously slipping into a role in the psyche of another person with whom he or she is currently involved.

The special thing about hypnosis is that the hypnotized person usually turns off his waking consciousness and with it his memory, and the hypnotist takes the place of the directing waking consciousness. The hypnotist can now talk to the hypnotized person's subconsciousness and in this way experience things that are otherwise inaccessible to the hypnotized person. He can also instruct him to do things, which the hypnotized person then performs.

Hypnosis attempts are one of the most direct ways of understanding the workings of the psyche because the hypnotist speaks directly to the subconscious mind of the hypnotized.

The words „relax – heavy – warm" that are used in hypnosis, describe the way from the waking consciousness to the subconsciousness. This way may be also found in deep relaxation or in the preparation for an astral journey.

A person in hypnosis is sometimes able to use telepathy far more precise then in the usual waking consciousness.

The agitation and propaganda of dictators and the like can in some cases be construed as virtually a form of mass hypnosis.

There is an interesting variant of hypnosis: remote hypnosis. After my magic teacher had been hypnotized by me a good 50 times, we came up with the idea of trying this at a distance. So, on the appointed evening, I stood in my room, drew the protective circle of the Lesser Pentagram Ritual and then concentrated on my magic teacher and hypnotized him in the same way as I did otherwise when we were together.

The next day I asked him what he had experienced. Of course, he didn't stay at home that night as we had arranged – he's more of an adventurer and found it boring at home and went to the pub. There, at the time I hypnotized him from a distance, he put his beer glass on an imaginary table and went home without a word, where he later "woke up" again after the hypnosis was over.

I imagined my magic teacher, because I assumed that he had stayed at home according to our appointment, in his room – this inner image of mine apparently called back him to his room. Fortunately, he has come across all roads unharmed …

3. d) Summary

The phenomena mentioned in this chapter show that with the help of dream journeys one can go with one's waking consciousness specifically into areas about which one wants to know something. Thus, one does not necessarily need a "monitor" like the pendulum, which displays the telepathically obtained information.

Collective telepathy shows that the psyche is apparently a complex structure in which the subconscious and the waking conscious can be separated. This enables the hypnotist to speak directly with the subconscious mind of the hypnotized – and in this way also to get telepathically acquired information through what the subconscious mind of the other says. In the middle of the last century this was a common method – it has been called "magician and medium".

The group dream journeys, the collective hypnosis and also the mass psychoses and the mass panic show that telepathy must probably be understood as a part of a larger network, in which the individual telepathic connection is, so to speak, a single thread.

4. Border Areas of Telepathy

First of all, telepathy seems to be something very simple and plain: "thought transmission". But the previous considerations have shown that on the one hand it is not only thoughts which are transmitted, but e.g. as in hypnosis also will, and on the other hand telepathy apparently also has a mode of operation and a concrete sequence in which it takes place (role of the subconsciousness). Finally, there seem to be other things connected with telepathy such as "successful wishing".

It is therefore useful to take a look at the peripheral areas of telepathy to see what could be related to telepathy, so that it becomes clearer what telepathy actually is and to which superordinate area it belongs.

4. a) Wishes

There is a special kind of desires which appear to telepathically invoke what is desired. This kind of wishes has similarities with the dream journeys where one searches for information that one suspects no one knows.

There seems to be something on the "telepathic level" that knows, for example, unknown healing possibilities and that can send you desired things.

Some years ago I once went down in the morning to the organic food store where I worked at that time and thought to myself that it would be nice to have a second bicycle to ride to the Rhine together with visitors of mine.

When I started to put the vegetables on the shelves of the health food store, a neighbor knocked on the shop window and asked me if I could use a bicycle, he wanted to give away one of his bikes. It was, of course, just the right size for me …

- - -

I regularly went to a meeting of owners of ecologic enterprises in Frankfurt. On my way way back I once thought that such meetings are quite helpful, but that I am actually looking for something else – someone with whom I can simply be together from heart to heart and where one does not have to explain anything long and wide.

Half an hour later I met a woman on the train, with whom I was later on also involved. As she told me at some point, she had wanted exactly the same thing as me on that day.

These almost unintentional, relaxed wishes pretty much always take half an hour to come true for me.

- - -

A couple I know was looking for a larger apartment for themselves and their children. While the woman read ads, phoned around, asked all her acquaintances about apartments, etc., her husband did nothing. At some point, she angrily told him that he probably thought the apartment would come to him on its own – to which he replied, "Yes, exactly."

A few days later, her landlord came by for a repair and told her how much he disliked placing ads for apartments he had to give away. When the two inquired what kind of apartment it was, it was just the right one …

- - -

Who does not know this: One calls someone and it is occupied. After you have tried again a while later, you find out that the other person also wanted to call you at exactly the same time and was therefore busy.

This does not sound like a coincidence …

4. b) <u>Omens and oracles</u>

If one lays Tarot cards or asks the I Ching, one receives quite meaningful answers. What is going on?

One possible explanation is that one first telepathically obtains the needed information, then telepathically selects the right cards, and then uses these cards as a "monitor" for the telepathically obtained information, which only becomes conscious by looking at the cards.

Most often this information becomes clearer when using the cards for a dream journey, that is, imagining going inwardly through the cards as through a door and then looking to see what one finds behind those cards.

- - -

In astrology, an explanation with the help of telepathy becomes more difficult, because the position of the planets is already known, from which one can derive, for example, the description of the character of a person, that is, his horoscope.

There is the same connection in astrology as in Tarot card reading, but the person is no longer the "active telepath". Instead, there is already a system of analogies that describes everything: the character of man corresponds to the planetary position at the time of his birth.

Is this analogy between character and planetary state something other than telepathy? Its similarity with Tarot card reading is great and also with dream journeys: One obtains information without having direct, material access to the source of the information.

If telepathy is simply described as the exchange of information between a person and something else, both telepathy and card reading and astrology fall under this definition.

The matter is even more complex, however, since astrology can also be used to describe the character of a company (founding horoscope) and also to predict the weather in the very long term ("hundred-year calendar" and the like).

These connections make a model that is not centered around the human being and his telepathy seem reasonable – that is, the model of a wide variety of non-material connections between all things, which in connection with the human being then appear as telepathy.

- - -

I was very sympathetic to a woman a few years ago – unfortunately she was already in a relationship. I wondered what would happen if I held back less. At that time I was standing in a meadow at the edge of a forest by an earth artwork that they had built (the woman and her friend are both sculptors).

When I asked myself this question, I was very strongly drawn to a ditch about 3m deep, through which the water from the forest flowed down into the valley during major rainstorms. I climbed down into this ditch and found three arrows there: two equal arrows right next to each other on the side of the creek where the earth artwork was, and a different looking arrow on the other side of the creek, which was missing the tip and had the notch for the string half broken.

The omen was not difficult to understand: The man was a Sagittarius (zodiac sign), so the arrow omen primarily referred to him – he was symbolically shooting the arrows. The same two arrows were in the ground on the artwork side of the creek, so they were the pair. The third arrow was me – on the other side of the creek, so separated from them. My arrow is missing the tip – impotent? My arrow is missing the half notch for the bowstring – incapable of action …

Can one wish for a clearer sign?

Again, there is more to this than telepathy. I asked for an answer, but it came not as a thought or inner image, but as an outer image. However, this outer and very prominent image (the three arrows) was already there before I asked my question. Also this experience can be explained more easily by a model of a "general network of connections between all things" than by a model of simple telepathy between two people.

Moreover, in this case the telepathy seems to spread not only spatially, but also temporally – the arrows were shot by someone and not found again before I asked my question and subsequently found the arrows as an answer to my question.

4. c) Telekinesis

In an earlier chapter I already told about my grandfather's experience with the healer, who was plucking a chicken, whose feathers then all flew to my grandfather when he entered the healer's house.

If you ask around, such events are not as rare and exotic as one could presume.

- - -

I once had a very impressive experience with my magic teacher, who wanted to summon a demon in his room. The demon did not come during this evocation (in contrast to other evcations), but something invisible hit a candle on a candlestick on the wall, whereupon this candle flew across the room.

- - -

You don't have to summon demons to experience telekinesis, though. There is also a simple experiment that anyone can perform and for which you can also find quite a few videos on the Internet under "Telekinesis Paper Spinning Top" or "PSI wheel".

The experiment setup is quite simple:

You take a small piece of cardboard as a foundation and stick a needle through it so that the tip sticks up.

Then you cut out a square piece of paper with a side length of 5-6cm from a type of paper with a hard surface – the hard surface can be recognized by the fact that it says "surface sized" on the package or by the fact that the paper is shiny; sometimes one side of a paper is shiny and the other dull. The smooth, hard, glossy surface of the paper further reduces the already low friction of the paper on the needle tip.

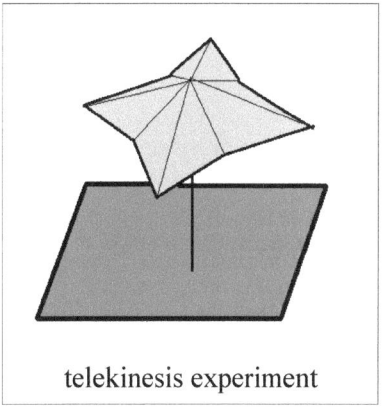

telekinesis experiment

Now the paper is folded four times and smoothed again so that there are four folds – two diagonals and the two "side center connecting" folds in between. The result is an eight-rayed star. Now fold the paper downwards at the diagonals and upwards at the "side center connecting ends". Now you can fold the paper by a little bend to a flat star, which has a ridge upwards at the diagonals and a valley downwards at the "side center connecting".

Now place the paper with its center on the point of the needle, checking by lightly bumping it to see if it sticks or if it turns effortlessly.

Now hold your hands next to the paper wheel and imagine that the wheel is turning. The usual direction of rotation is towards the fingertips. Therefore, you should place your right hand behind the wheel with the fingertips pointing to the left and your left hand in front of the wheel with the fingertips pointing to the right – the fingertips are now both pointing counterclockwise. Of course, you can do the same thing with your hands facing clockwise.

It is recommended to do this experiment yourself to experience the turning yourself and not just read in a book or see in a video that it is possible.

This experiment clearly shows that what is found in the research of telepathy is more than just telepathy – it is not only a "perception without physical contact" possible, but also an "action without physical contact".

The background of telepathy thus becomes larger and larger – telepathy is not an isolated phenomenon, but a single phenomenon occurring within a much larger, complex web of non-physical contexts.

- - -

Telekinesis is, of course, at its simplest when only a very small mass needs to be moved with telekinesis, i.e. only a very small force needs to be applied for an effect to occur – like the electrical charges in computers, for example.

This makes PCs quite susceptible to the moods of their users …

- - -

Just as telepathy can be coordinated between several people e.g. on dream journeys, telekinesis can be coordinated between several people e.g. in the paper wheel experiment.

Possibly there are also unintentional cases of a coordination of telepathy and/or telekinesis:

Once when I was a tour guide in Egypt, I took my son with me. In the Horus temple of Edfu we both stood in such places that we formed an equilateral triangle with the pedestal of the Horus statue (which, however, was no longer there), and we both concentrated on Horus. When a woman passed through this triangle, she fainted when she arrived at the center of this triangle.

Of course, I don't know if this was really due to the energy of David and me and possibly Horus as well, but the woman fainting was quite a striking event – and David and I felt quite a bit of energy when invoking Horus at that moment.

4. d)   Astral projection

Astral projection is the oldest and most important religious experience, which ultimately even gave rise to religion.

During an astral projection one leaves one's own physical body and floats above it and can largely move freely, walk through walls, look at everything and so on. While doing so, one does not have a material body, but sometimes still has a bodily sensation, which, however, is different from the normal bodily sensation.

Such astral projection occur most often in life-threatening situations in which one can see no escape – a so-called "near-death experience".

These astral projection have already been depicted in cave paintings and also in most ancient cultures. Because of this "floating" of the astral body, the soul has been compared to a bird all over the world and therefore has been depicted as a bird, a bird with a human head, a human with a bird's head, a human with feathers, a human with wings (angels) and so on – the soul-bird.

Through the experience of astral projection during a near-death, people already knew in the Stone Age that there is more than just the physical body. This gave rise to the image of the soul bird, then the otherworld with the souls of the dead, the otherworld journey of the shamans, the cult of the dead, the gods, and so on.

Of course, astral projections do not only occur in near-death experiences – they are only particularly frequent and also conscious in this context. There are also people who have always been able to leave their body from childhood. And it is possible to learn astral projection even without death-threatening situations.

Astral projection is one of the experiences that have an effect on one's own conception of the world only when one has experienced it oneself. One can also experience it deliberately, but the instructions for this would fill a book of its own (see "Astral Projection for Beginners" if you like).

Astral projection shows that you can leave your own body with your consciousness or at least with your perception. During this process you don't need a monitor anymore and you don't perceive only diffuse and blurred telepathically received thoughts, but you are in the telepathic perception with your consciousness. One can go with his astral body into the neighboring room and look around there.

This astral body is obviously what perceives telepathically. If you leave your own body with it, you can look at what is on the table in the neighboring room – you could then call this fully conscious, sovereign telepathy.

This astral body also seems to be connected with the subconsciousness – at least it is normally as subconscious as the "organ" which receives the telepathic information. Whether the astral body and the subconscious are identical with each other is not sure at first, but they are at least on the same level.

In telepathy one receives information from this level, in dream journeys one consciously goes into this level and searches for information there, and in astral projection one is consciously able to perceive and act on this level.

In a dream journey, one is in a world of images similar to dreams, but on which one can obtain concrete, accurate information – just as dreams are also very accurate when one has learned to understand their images.

In an astral projection, on the other hand, one perceives the world as if with the physical senses.

In a dream journey one sends out or expands one's perceptive faculty, but remains with one's consciousness in one's own body – in an astral projection one leaves one's own body with one's consciousness and with one's perceptive faculty and goes to a place which one can then look at.

The perspectives in a dream journey and in an astral projection are consequently different. One could say as a working hypothesis that in dream travel one looks at things "from within" and "from a distance" and in astral projection one looks at things "from without" and "from close up". In dream travel one remains in one's body – in astral projection one leaves it.

4. e) Magic

The whole field of magic is too large to be presented here. In very simplified terms, magic is the ability to wish for something in a way that causes the fulfillment of those wishes.

There are many rules and tools for this, ranging from positive thinking to amulets, talismans, symbols, sacrifices, rituals, and the invocation of deities.

Ultimately, magic is nothing more than the almost purposeless wishing, which has already been described in an earlier chapter (bicycle wished). The relaxed intention, the serenity and the trust are what brings about the wish fulfillment.

Magic can be defined roughly as "systemetic appliance of telepathy and telekinesis".

4. f) Poltergeists

Poltergeists are a very special and impressive form of telekinesis and therefore also belong to the border area of telepathy.

- - -

When I was about 23 years old, I was once sitting alone in my room in my parents' house when I heard footsteps approaching our front door. Suddenly it struck me that I had never heard that before. Then someone opened the front door without using a key, even though I knew the door was locked, and came up the stairs – a somewhat ponderous man's step that I didn't know. My hair stood on end …

Then he stopped for a moment in front of my door and then went across the corridor to my sister's room – again without unlocking it. So I mustered up my courage and checked to see if my sisters room was really locked – it was. I got the key and searched the room – no one there. When my parents and siblings came back, I didn't tell them.

A few days later, however, my siblings started telling me that they kept hearing someone running up the stairs. That's when I told them my experience, too. This went on for about three quarters of a year and after a while we got used to "him".

Sometimes "he" also came when we had visitors. When the visitor asked who was running up the stairs, we answered "Oh, that's just our poltergeist".

It was a bit disturbing that the poltergeist sometimes stood (invisibly) next to the bed of one of one my sisters during the night and told her something – that disturbs the sleep a little bit …

Only my father thought that all this was complete nonsense and scolded us quite a bit. As I was told, the others were sitting together one Sunday morning at breakfast when a tremendous noise broke out in my room – as if I were smashing all the furniture with an axe. My father angrily stomped up to my room, which was above the living room where everyone was eating, but came back down shortly afterwards rather meekly and said that there was no one up there – I hadn't been home at all. From then on, my father also convinced of the existence of "our" poltergeist.

- - -

Probably one can understand poltergeists most likely as the astral body of a deceased – perhaps however also as that of a living one. There may also be several possible causes for this phenomenon.

Whether the attempts of the poltergeist to talk to one of my sisters were actually external-acoustic or whether they took place telepathically cannot be clearly decided. However, the "poltergeist", that is, the running on the stairs, was either acoustically-normal to all who heard it, or so intensely and realistically telepathic that no one noticed the difference from normal hearing.

- - -

In the beginning, I sometimes could not clearly distinguish normal perceptions and telepathic perceptions either. For example, once when I went to my magic teacher's house in the woods, I heard him calling loudly, but could not see him anywhere.

When I then arrived at his house, he told me that he had concentrated on me to cancel, because he had already drunk too much to be able to do any experiments.

Thereupon I looked for a possibility to distinguish telepathically received thoughts from my own thoughts and from external words. I found a way quite soon:

> Telepathically received thoughts have no roots in me, I cannot see where they come from – a thought of my own, on the other hand, I can always trace back at least a little bit.

> The outer hearing is distanced, one perceives something new, foreign on the outside – the inner hearing feels as if one would find something familiar, known, although it is also new, because at its perception (like a memory) it is already inside oneself.

With a little practice, the distinction between one's own thoughts, telepathically received thoughts and externally spoken words may become quite easy and quite reliable.

4. g) Homeopathy

In homeopathy, something strange actually happens: you mix a substance more and more with milk sugar until finally there is almost nothing left of the original substance in the mixture. Then you give some of this special lactose to a person who has an ailment that would be caused in a healthy person by just this lactose mixture.

At the very least, you can say that the substance that you have mixed with the large amounts of lactose is not what is effective in the homeopathic remedy. It is rather the information about the original substance that is still in the lactose of this remedy that is effective.

This relation of the original substance to the lactose mixture is very reminiscent of the relation between the waking consciousness and the subconsciousness, and even more of the relation between the physical body and the astral body: in the homoeopathic remedy there is only the astral body of the original substance. Since the astral body is the "place" or the "body" of telepathy, the lactose, to which the astral body of the original substance still adheres, can also telepathically give the patient the information he needs. Homeopathy is therefore telepathic healing.

Telepathy appears in homeopathy also in another place: When a patient asks the homeopath for a remedy, the remedy begins to work not when the patient takes it, but when the homeopath has decided which remedy to give the patient.

I have experienced this myself several times when my friend Jörg, who is a homeopath, had chosen a remedy for me.

Telepathy goes even further in homeopathy. A student of homeopathy once fell ill in South America and could not help himself. During a telephone conversation with his teacher, the teacher told him which homeopathic remedy to take. However, it was impossible for the student to get this remedy in South America in the remote area where he was.

On a second call, the teacher told him to write the name of the remedy on a piece of paper, pour water over it, and then drink the water. This worked just as well as the remedy itself – it seems that taking the globules is not about taking a substance, but about connecting with the astral body of this substance through a decision and an action.

In the previous example, where the effect begins at the moment when the homeopath has decided on a remedy, the patient's intention to also take this remedy as soon as he receives it is the "contract" with the astral body of this remedy.

The method of "pouring water over slips of paper" is already at least 4000 years old. In the villages of ancient Egypt, in the village square or near the temple, there was a statue of the young falcon god Horus, who stood with one foot on a snake or crocodile and with the other on a scorpion. This statue-group stood in the middle of a small basin with a spout.

Now, if someone was bitten by a scorpion or a snake, the healing consisted essentially of pouring water over this statue, catching it with a cup in front of the spout, and then giving this water to the bitten person to drink – then the bitten person was healed in the same way as the goddess Isis healed her son Horus from such bites.

Until the Middle Ages, it was common practice in Christianity to drink water from the skull bowls of the saints who protected people from the illness, for the healing of which the specific saint was responsible. This custom is also known from the Germanic tribes, the Tibetans, the Neolithic hunters in Great Britain and others.

For today's feeling this method, in which the sick person is healed by a telepathic ("magic") connection to a healing saint, is possibly rather old-fashioned …

4. h) <u>Materializations</u>

Materializations are probably the magical phenomenon that can most violently shake the scientific worldview that is mostly common today.

In spiritualistic sessions materializations are quite a common phenomenon – usually chocolate bars and similar quite normal things appear on the table between the participants. Also in Wiccan rituals ("witch cult") it happens that suddenly something is lying on the altar, which was not there before.

This story about a materialization starts with the fact that I was hiking on the Canary Island La Palma and felt the need to wear a necklace. I asked myself which necklace would be the right one – the pendant would have to reflect my own being and it would have to be made of gold and the pendant should not be too big.

When I got to the beach, I sat down on a rock that was a three feet high and sometimes had waves crashing against it at the bottom. After I had been sitting there for a while, a high wave came up to me. Then I saw something golden flashing in the spray on the rock between my feet and quickly grabbed it.

It was a golden, artfully twisted chain with a golden Christ as a pendant, who had raised his arms as if in an invocation – but he was not hanging on the cross (which I don't like at all). I didn't know what to say anymore, when I realized that I was holding in my hands exactly the necklace I had wished for shortly before – and that the sea had thrown it to me with a high wave …

When I called my friend a little later, she told me that at the same time I found the necklace, she had spontaneously bought a large painting of Christ in an antique store – and Christ had never been a big topic in our conversations otherwise.

About a year later, I had a major crisis and wondered what to do next. Finally I came to the conclusion that I really have to let go of everything completely, so that what I really am can show itself. At that time I was in Offenburg visiting the friend I just mentioned.

I was standing at a traffic island in the middle of an intersection, where this traffic island was set up as a crosswalk – you could walk into the middle from all sides and from there to where you wanted to go. This small circular square in the middle of the traffic island is surrounded all around by about eight upright stones about the height of a man – a "mini Stonehenge". So I went to one of those stones and squatted down in front of it and took off my gold Christ necklace from La Palma and my silver dragon necklace, both of which I wore all the time at those days, and put them on the ground in front of the stone and said, "For the one for whom they are intended." Then I looked at them for a moment and left.

About three months later I was traveling from Freiburg to Bonn and had a one and a half hour stop at the Offenburg train station. Something drew me to the stone circle on the traffic island and although I told myself that it was silly and sentimental to think of my two necklaces, I followed the impulse and went there. When I got there, I squatted down in front of the stone where I had laid down my two necklaces. Of course, they were not there anymore – gold and silver do not stay long in a busy public place like that …

I was a little sad that I no longer had the two necklaces. When I wanted to get up and go again, I looked again at the foot of the stone – and suddenly my two necklaces were there again. I can hardly describe how that felt. That was actually not possible – that was really magic or something even greater.

Either the two necklaces had just materialized again (and "dematerialized" before) or the two chains had been invisible for three months. Materialization seems more likely to me, since the place was very clean and had obviously been swept regularly and all weeds and the like removed.

Materialization apparently involves something that clearly goes beyond telepathy and telekinesis, but belongs to the same realm. I have examined this phenomenon in more detail in my book "Die Magie-Formel".

4. i) The ABC of the Sorcerer's Apprentice

As already Goethe described in his poem "The Sorcerer's Apprentice", it is problematic to learn only a part of the whole knowledge about a subject. This is also the case with real magic. It makes sense, for example, to develop perceptive ability and action ability in roughly equal measure.

If you can perceive telepathically a great deal and, for example, feel all the feelings of the people around you, you will be flooded with these feelings and can become completely helpless and even incapacitated. So the ability to act is needed, which here means that one can draw an effective line between inside and outside. Therefore, as a sorcerer's apprentice, one first learns to create a protective circle – for example, with the Lesser Pentagram Ritual.

There is also the reverse case of the magician who only cared about getting more and more power, being able to wish more and more effectively, being able to hypnotize everyone at will, etc. Here the danger exists that the person concerned causes many effects by the way, which he did not want to reach at all – simply because he does a lot, but sees little. Here a somewhat clearer perception would be helpful, allowing one to hit the door and not the wall when walking.

It is generally useful to find a balance between connection and disconnection. If one is a counselor, for example, it is useful to always imaginatively have a table between oneself and the person seeking counseling, and to put everything the person seeking counseling says on that table – rather than letting it come into oneself.

Telepathy is not only an exchange of information – it is also an exchange of life force. Again, this is probably best explained by an example:

I noticed during my visits to my magic teacher after some time that he started to get tired at 10:30PM, while I became more and more awake. This surprised me, but I didn't think anything more of it.

After a few weeks, however, something strange happened. It was once again about 10:30PM and my magic teacher was getting tired as usual. Then I suddenly got a strong craving for a bottle of beer and almost got up to take a bottle that was on the shelf. But then it struck me that I don't like beer at all and never drink alcohol because I don't like the taste or the effect.

That's when I combined both phenomena – apparently I drained life force from my teacher, making him tired and me frisky, and with his life force I naturally absorbed his alcoholism and suddenly had a craving for beer. This craving can be really intense … I had not known that before.

This is the same phenomenon as in homeopathy: I absorb something from the astral body of the other person, which for the sake of simplicity I will call "life force" here, and thus also take over the properties of this astral body. In the case of homeopathy this effect is desirable, in the case of alcoholism it was rather unpleasant – fortunately it had no lasting effect.

I then also learned quite quickly to stop unconsciously sucking life force – since then I am no longer an "energy vampire". My magic teacher and I have since then always had the feeling at about the same time that it is enough for today.

This "vampire effect" can be observed in many places: When one is dominant in a conversation and does most of the talking, this person becomes more and more powerful and the others more and more tired. This effect is also seen when one gets his way and the others give in: The commitment to the subject and its emotional importance determine how much life force the participants give as a stake in the dispute – and the winner of the dispute receives all the life force, all the stake of all the participants. You can see this in the way the winner radiates …

4. j) Summary

The border areas of telepathy show that telepathy is only a single phenomenon in a much broader web of connections and effects.

Omens and oracles show as a picture the answer to the question asked telepathically.

Wishes have effects, which is systematically applied in magic.

In telekinesis and poltergeist apparitions, a physical effect of a non-physical cause occurs.

With the materialization even matter arises due to a wish or the like or the matter appears spontaneously at a place.

In astral projection, the waking mind has become consciousof that part of one's own being from which telepathy (and probably also telekinesis) emanates.

In homeopathy, a telepathic bond is formed with a substance outside (remedy) or a part of the astral body of this substance is absorbed into one's own astral body.

Also the "life force vampirism" can be understood as the "robbing" of a part of the astral body (life force) of another person.

5. The Content of the "Telepathic Transmission"

The phenomena considered so far clearly show that in telepathy not only thoughts are transmitted:

> Thoughts, images and feelings can be sent and received;
>
> it is possible to extract "life force" from another (winning an argument; pushing someone into a role, energy vampirism);
>
> feelings and needs can be transmitted (thirst for beer);
>
> it is possible to telepathically exerted will (remote hypnosis);
>
> an event can be telepathically summoned (fulfillment of a wish; receiving an omen as an answer to a question).

With the help of telepathy the whole spectrum of psychic impulses can be sent and received: thoughts, images, feelings, needs (beer example), will and life force (parts of the astral body).

In telepathy, a connection is made with another person or with something else that contains all the elements found in the psyche – so the psyche of one person is connected with the psyche of another person or with the "psyche" of something else (for example, in homeopathy).

The area described as "psyche" and also the area capable of telepathy can be perceived directly during astral projection as the astral body. Consequently, the processes during telepathy can be most elegantly be described as contacts of two astral bodies.

As the examples given in the earlier chapters show, this astral body contact can lead not only to perceptions but also to effects: telekinesis.

To put it simply, these effects can be understood as the extension of one's own astral body to the physical body or to the astral body of another person, whereby the one who has extended his astral body can direct the physical body of the one to whom he has extended his consciousness (astral body) in the same way as he can direct his own body.

This description corresponds exactly to the process in hypnosis and also to the feeling one has when hypnotizing someone.

For the sake of simplicity, the substance of the astral body, and therefore the substance of which telepathic messages are composed, will be called "life force" in the following.

6. Special Forms of Telepathy

There are still some more special forms of telepathy which have not been described so far. They can further clarify and complement what has been presented so far.

6. a) Automatic writing

Automatic writing is very similar to scrying. The only difference is that one does not unconsciously move a pendulum with the arm and hand, but a pen on a sheet of paper. Both the pendulum and the pen are a "monitor" for the telepathically received messages.

If you want to learn automatic writing, it is best to sit down at a table with a pen in your hand and place a sheet of paper in front of you. Then you put the tip of the pen on the paper and tell your arm to write. He will probably just twitch or scribble at first, perhaps making some kind of "abstract drawing." As a rule, automatic writing is easier if one has practiced commuting first – the required movements of the arm and hand for commuting are smaller and less complex …

When you practice automatic writing for a while, several things may happen: your hand starts writing, or you hear words inside, or you wordlessly "feel" some information.

At this point at the latest, one should ask questions to open a conversation. Sometimes automatic writing also only gets going when one asks a question with great emphasis or suffering, e.g., "Damn it, what is this strange life all about!!?"

The feelings are, so to speak, the postage stamp on the telepathic letter …

A variant of automatic writing is automatic speaking. Here you ask yourself a question and then listen to what you spontaneously answer yourself. In this way one can also address individual organs or chakras within oneself or gods and saints.

Pendulums, dream journeys, automatic writing, automatic speaking, etc. are all different methods, but they are all tools to establish the connection between the waking consciousness and the subconsciousness, i.e. the astral body, and thus to telepathy. With practice, after a while, these methods cease to be clearly delineated methods – one becomes capable of making contact and one can use any method. The method itself recedes into the background and the ability to make that connection comes to the fore.

Automatic speaking is described in the Bible as "speaking in tongues", that is, speaking in different languages that one has never learned. I have also experienced a similar effect and have been told about it by others. When you are abroad and listening in a certain "unfocused" way, you seem to telepathically perceive the content of the words of the foreign language you don't understand and translate them into your own language.

The first time I experienced this, I was a little confused (two men were talking about me), but since I heard from others that they had also experienced like things, it was easier for me to accept that this strange phenomenon exists.

"Speaking in tongues" is the inversion of this process: one taps telepathically into the foreign language, translates what one wants to say into this language and then speaks it out. However, I have not yet experienced this myself. I have heard only once in Egypt at the lake Birket Karun someone "speaking in tongues" – since I and also the others could not understand the language, however, it could not be checked whether this language had really a content. I was only quite sure that it was not ancient Egyptian (which I studied at that time).

From all this it follows that telepathy is not language-bound. Telepathy transmits a content, but not concrete words. There is apparently a translation mechanism in the astral body that has access to the language center and the "database" in the brain and can therefore translate the telepathic information into the language of the receiver. When "speaking in tongues" even the speaker seems to be able to tap into the speech center of the listener and use his vocabulary.

6. b) The "cloak of invisibility"

In an earlier chapter I already told about the telepathy contests with my son, who by his telepathic concentration made me say "Sydney" when asked for the capital of Australia.

We once did a similar game while walking through the fields to the train station. David, who was then 9 or 10 years old, was hiding and I was looking for him. That's when I got the idea to look for him telepathically – however, David had also gotten the idea to hide himself telepathically … But that made things easier for me in the end: I only had to look for the place where a kind of fog hid my view and where I got the feeling, that I should not look at that place. In this way, I found David immediately.

A few years ago I discovered that the Germanic seers also knew this effect. In the "Saga of Hrolf Kraki and his Berserks" it is described that a Jarl (Count) hid the two sons of the king, who had been killed by a conqueror, on the Jarl's island. So that no one would find the sons, he put a spell over the island – which, however, was noticed by the Conqueror-King's sorcerer-seers.

The saga says about it:

> *Then he sent for seers from all over the land – sorceresses and sorcerers – and ordered them to search the entire land from front to back, from left to right, all the islands and all the far out skerries* (low-land islands)*, but they could not find the two sons.*
> *So he sent for magicians who could see everything they wanted, and they told him that the boys were not raised anywhere in the land, but that they were not far away either.*
> *King Frodi said, "We have searched far and wide for them, so it is very unlikely that they are near, but there is another island not far away where we have not taken any particular trouble, because no one lives there – well, no one except a peasant, a poor starveling."*
> *"Look there first," said the Galdr-man* (wizard)*, "for there is a dense fog over that island, and we cannot well see what lies around that man's farm. It seems to us that this man is skillful and that he is more than he appears to be."*

I had to grin very broadly when I discovered this text, for that is exactly what I expierienced with David …

6. c)   Transference of Consciousness

There are a lot of practical applications of telepathy. One, for example, is searching for lost things. I have been asked many times for help with lost house keys, purses, laptops, etc.

The method that seems to be the most effective, at least for me, is to have the object described to me and then imagine that I am crossing over into this object, i.e. that I transfere my consciousness into this object.

Then the first thing I do is look at what the environment of this object looks like – cloth?, wood?, earth?, dusty?, damp? etc. Then I expand my consciousness a bit further and look at the environment of what is directly surrounding the object. Thereby I see e.g. a doormat in a car behind the driver's seat (there lay a wallet) or a pocket at a guitar case in a room (there lay a front door key). Usually this is enough for the person who lost the item to know where to look.

This method can also be used, for example, to find the fault in a car engine. One makes a dream journey, so to speak, into the engine of the car in question and looks to see if one can find wobbly spots, breaks, or the like. Sometimes it also helps to imagine the engine in operation and then look at the energy flows in it. In this way I once discovered that the axle of the alternator was worn out and therefore was wobbling and could not produce enough power anymore.

So dream journeys can have a very practical use …

There are almost unlimited applications for these forms of telepathy. For example, a good acquaintance of mine once had a very important appointment with a banker. I offered to help him if he could get me a photo of this banker. I then used this photo to describe the general character of the banker and his values and ways of doing things. This seemed to me to be still justifiable and not too transgressive – and it helped my acquaintance a lot in his negotiations.

This photo method is also commonly used by people who telepathically search for missing persons. They can sometimes tell with the first glance at the photo whether the missing person is still alive or not. In Cyprus, for example, some young people had the joke of going to the seer Daskalos and showing him a photo of a friend of theirs who had been left outside in a car, and asking Daskalos to look for him. Then Daskalos got quite angry and told them that the one they were looking for was sitting outside in the car and that they should leave right away.

The astonishingly great certainty that one can attain in telepathy can also be judged by an experience of an acquaintance with the seer Buchela, whose abilities the German chancellor Konrad Adenauer often made use of. My acquaintance went to Buchela to ask her advice about a problem. During her consultation she mentioned the four siblings of my acquaintance, whereupon he contradicted and said that he had only three siblings.

Buchela got angry and replied that he had four siblings when she said that. Then he remembered that he had another sister who died at birth and was never counted …

I also once spoke to Buchela on the phone myself and was quite impressed by her clarity and decisiveness.

When someone comes to me for advice about an illness or a psychological problem, I sometimes ask to be allowed to transfer my consciousness into the body of the person seeking advice, so that I can take a look around.

For this purpose I imagine to go out of my body with my consciousness and to enter the body of the other person. Usually I start by going through the seven main chakras of the person from top to bottom and look at their condition, as this shows me the general condition of the person seeking advice.

If someone has a specific ailment, I also look at the corresponding organ.

In the meantime I have found out that it is very effective to ask a question aloud to the organ in question and then to let it have my voice, i.e. to go into automatic speech.

This is quite fun in a way, because these organs are all quite emotional and speak in ways that I would never speak otherwise. And what the organs say is always quite clear and unmistakable …

A good acquaintance of mine now makes such "automatic conversations" with her organs, chakras and with the planets in her horoscope almost daily.

This variant of telepathy is extremely useful and can quickly become something completely normal.

This form of transference of consciousness can also be used when someone is panicked or on the verge of a panic attack or can't get out of a crying fit. In these cases, almost all of the person's life force is congested in their upper three chakras and the lower three chakras are largely empty.

If one then directs some of the life force back down, slows down the frantically spinning upper chakras and restarts the almost still lower chakras, the panic and crying fit will stop after a while.

Of course, these are all things that you have to try out and experience for yourself to see that they are actually possible and work.

In Tibet, in the "Six Yogas of Naropa", there is a meditation that enables a dying yogi or lama to take his consciousness out of his body (astral projection), to search for the body of a young person who has just died, to revive this body by contacting it with his own astral body, and then to inhabit this body, that is, to continue living with the old consciousness in a new body.

However, this sixth yoga meditation of Naropa, called "Phowa", now really does not belong in a book with the title "Telepathy for Beginners", but in a book with the title "Telepathy for Advanced Students" …

This Phowa has become common knowledge since a few years: In the last scene of the movie "Avatar" the consciousness of Jack Sully is transferred from his human body to his new Na'vi body with the help of a ritual.

6. d) Time telepathy

True dreams are dreams in which one dreams something, which then comes true – usually the next day. Such dreams are quite common, as you can find out once you start talking to other people about such things.

One can also look into the future with intention – as this is known from the seers and visionaries of almost all peoples.

The process itself is simple: you sit down and look inwardly toward the future.

Inwardly you can use a calendar or the image of a year circle or similar. However, these pictures are not absolutely necessary – they help, however, with the temporal orientation in the future.

The inner activity during this "looking into the future" feels quite similar to trying to remember something you know you know, but have just forgotten. In this "remembering" one is merely looking "in the other direction", that is, into the future.

In this way, for example, I have seen when I will meet my future wife and what we will do together first. Since the date was at the end of July and I had looked into the future at New Year's Eve, I had to wait a while … When I still didn't know three days before the foreseen common vacation who it should be that comes along, I began to doubt, but the evening before my departure she then contacted me and said that she wants to come along.

This possibility of looking into the future raises two questions – one very practical and one theoretical.

The practical question is whether it is beneficial in a situation to know the future. Sometimes there are circumstances in which this helps - for example, in depression, when one can see its end or pleasing events in the near future. Sometimes one is also faced with the question of which path to take – here, too, a look into the future can sometimes help to clarify things.

The theoretical question is, what would be the nature of the world if it is possible to foresee the future. This question is quite similar to the one that arises from the functioning of astrology, with the help of which one can already say now what character a person will have who is born in Berlin on January 1, 2304 at 1.15PM. Also in this respect the future is already fixed and can be described with the help of astrology precisely and in detail.

I have examined this question etc. in detail in my book "Reincarnation". For the telepathy considered in this book it is enough to know that telepathy reaches not only to other people and also not only to distant places and into the past, but also into the future.

There are also professionals of "time telepathy": the Tibetan tulkus. These are the approximately 1000 lamas, that is, monks who are so advanced that they can, on the one hand, remember their previous lifes and, on the other hand, predict their next incarnation.

The monks of the monastery to which a deceased tulku belonged then search for a child matching the tulku's description at the time predicted by the tulku in the place he or she named. Then two rehearsals are conducted: First, the child is presented with a few items, which include a few items that belonged to the tulku, and second, the child is asked basic questions about the Tibetan religion and the various meditations the tulku used in his previous life.

If the child recognizes the items he possessed in his previous incarnation as a tulku, and can also correctly answer the monks' questions about the meditations, it is considered proven that the child is indeed the reincarnated tulku. He then returns to the monastery as a child and is trained there, i.e. his knowledge and abilities are reawakened.

By this system, in Tibet it always happens that children are abbots of a monastery – they are reincarnated monks who can remember their previous lives through time telepathy and are therefore, so to speak, very old adults in the bodies of children.

6. e) Sending and receiving

There is one more aspect of telepathy that is worth looking at. So far, there has always been talk of a sender and a receiver. However, it is questionable whether this is really precise in this way.

If only because the future is predictable and describable by astrology or by tarot cards, the question arises whether there is not rather a great "astral body organism" encompassing the whole world, in which the astral bodies of the individual human beings are, so to speak, a single cell and which vibrates in an "overall rhythm" which coordinates all its components with each other.

There is also the observation that a needy addict and a helpful ascetic attract each other. The same is true for the powerless victim and the power-hungry perpetrator, and likewise for the star with delusions of grandeur and the fan with an inferiority complex.

One can, of course, say that the act comes from the perpetrator and the victim is the sufferer, but they are both so dependent on each other that one should rather say that they are the two halves of the same sorrowful drama.

Of course, this does not change the guilt of the perpetrator in his deeds – but it shows that the victim must also change if he does not want to remain a victim.

Also with telepathy it is not always clear where the cause actually lies – did I send out that I had no desire to meet the other person or did the other person have no desire and I felt that?

It seems to be at least more cautious to speak for practical reasons about someone who telepathically "speaks" and about someone who telepathically "hears", but not to consider this as a causal connection.

Causal connections first of all belong to the physical world – astrology and oracles like the tarot are not causal connections, but analogies, i.e. correspondences.

A telepathic connection also needs for its explanation only the touch of the two people who have this connection, so to speak the "contact of their astral bodies". The whole magic is based on such analogies, correspondences and "meaningful coincidences".

Such "telepathic couplings" can be very complex. For example, my friend Jörg and I met every two weeks for decades to do dream journeys, family constellations, and the like. In doing so, we noticed that we basically always experienced the same thing during the past two weeks. This went down to the details – I had felt the need to put a yellow rose on my home altar, and when Jörg came he had to laugh because he had of course done the same thing. Eventually we came to look at our two accounts of the last two weeks like the narrative of one and the same person – so there was more clarity about what was going on in our lives.

Obviously there is a complex "telepathic coupling" between Jörg and me, which is much easier to describe if one simply speaks of a simultaneity and an analogy and not of a causing sender and an influenced receiver.

For about half a year this Jörg/Harry system expanded to five more people who were, so to speak, "all swimming in the same river" and whose experiences coincided and complemented each other.

This has been a very pleasant experience …

6. f) Sensitive computers

The tiny electrical charges that store the information in computers and that process the data in them make the PCs very sensitive – you don't need a large amount of "telekinetic power" to change a few electronically stored data or an electronic process.

I know a woman near whom almost every PC crashes – but if she moves more than 4m away from the PC, it starts up again and works normally. This is far from being an isolated case.

My son David and I once tried to telekinetically repair a PC of mine that had some problems a few years ago. I can only advise against this procedure, because during this "healing" the processor of my PC burned out – too much telekinetic energy …

Even the internet can be tapped telepathically. It happens to me quite often that when I turn on my PC I already know that today I will find a certain information, invoice or the like in my e-mails.

6. g) Summary

That which is called "astral body" in humans and has the ability of telepathy is not only present in humans, but also in animals, plants and minerals (as shown among others by the photo experiment and homeopathy). All things have an astral body and can be contacted telepathically.

Moreover, these astral bodies can also act on each other (telekinesis, hypnosis, homeopathy).

Finally, the comprehensive "astral body of the world" seems to reach into the past and into the future, so that one can also see the future on the level of the astral body, i.e. by "time telepathy".

A single act of telepathy is obviously a small movement, a small connection in a big whole. The part of a single person in this big whole is his astral body. This astral body is that which can telepathically send and receive something.

The "astral body of the world" behaves like an organism, in which all parts are coupled with each other by analogies and which vibrate with each other. They become visible among other things in astrology and in other oracles. Telepathy could therefore be an analogy phenomenon and not a causal effect – i.e. a two-way connection rather than an influence.

This would also explain why telepathy cannot be explained in a physical-causal way, i.e. on a material level …

7. Telepathy in the Horoscope

In the many horoscopes I have interpreted in the course of time, I have noticed that in most people who have a pronounced talent for telepathy and the like, and in whose lives telepathy is something normal without any practice, there is often an aspect between the Moon and Neptune – usually a conjunction, a trine or a sextile. These are the three harmonically conjunct relationships between two planets.

This observation fits the previous considerations about telepathy, because the Moon in the horoscope represents, among other things, the subconsciousness, the life force and the astral body, which, according to the previous considerations in this book, seems to be the "place of telepathy".

Neptune is the planet that represents the dissolution of boundaries, the "swinging together" and the connections in the big picture.

The three aspects conjunction, trine and sextile represent three forms of connections, that is, they connect the Moon to Neptune. As a result, Neptune dissolves the boundaries of the Moon – the astral body becomes open, sociable, and thus receptive to telepathic impressions.

If Mars is added to this Moon-Neptune aspect (with largely any aspect), this Moon-Neptune combination receives the power of Mars in addition, which, according to my observations so far, significantly increases the talent for telepathic transmission.

Of course, this does not mean that one is "telepathically capable" only with these aspects in the horoscope, but only that one then has a special tendency to telepathy.

I myself have none of these aspects and have still experienced telepathy – but I have had to either practice for a long time for most things, or search for a way that would allow me to do the things I was aiming for.

On the occasions when I have done the "postcard experiment" with a larger number of people, all have been able to see parts of the image on the postcard. A suitable frame enables just about everyone to experience telepathy.

However, the increased telepathic ability with a Moon-Neptune aspect in the horoscope still shows that the telepathy model outlined so far in this book is accurate.

Since Moon and Neptune are the two "sensitive" planets, one could assume that telepathy occurs mainly in "sensitive plants" – which is not completely wrong. But this by no means rules out the possibility that a sober scientist or an enthusiastic athlete may also have a great talent for telepathy – after all, the Moon and Neptune can be well integrated into the overall character. For example, my son is both a researcher/scientist and an athlete (parkour coach and ninja warrior on the RTL show) and has considerable talents of telepathy and telekinesis.

So telepathy and telekinesis don't have to be indicative of a hypersensitive, out-of-touch-with-reality character.
Both abilities are eminently suitable for everyday life.

8. Telepathy Models

There are already some telepathy models – the best known are the life force model and the information model.

In general it can be said that man tends to explain the unknown with the known. This is simply the way the brain works: one understands the unknown by relating it to the known. "Understanding" ultimately simply means that one has found a coherent overall description.

Thus the light was explained around 1700 with the "ether", which was an auxiliary construction of the physics of that time – this concept was then taken up again around 1900 for the explanation of telepathy. This ether corresponds from its description to a large extent to the life force.

At present the information model is quite popular, which is an analogy to the PCs and the Internet.

Going back even further to the Middle Ages, telepathy was explained in terms of the Holy Spirit.

In cultures with a mythological-magical worldview, it is the spirits of the dead and the gods that bring about telepathy and magic in general.

In view of this human tendency to explain the unknown with what is known in each case from the current world view, one should be careful with any kind of explanation. Of course, it is at the basis of every understanding that one connects new observations with already known observations – understanding is essentially recognizing.

However, it might be appropriate, instead of a hasty classification of the unknown into the known, to take a lot of time for experiments, a precise observation and a precise description – if only because this procedure ultimately leads to expertise and thus has the greatest benefit. In this way, one can also arrive at new and more comprehensive models – just as Einstein was only able to develop the theory of relativity because he looked at what the observations showed and was prepared to simply draw the conclusions from them, even if they led into completely new territory.

This procedure can also sometimes mean that one observes something, which one cannot connect with something known yet and which therefore remains provided with a more or less large "?" in the own world view.

But an honest "?" is always better than an only asserted "!" or a thoughtlessly accepted "." …

9. Telepathy in Everyday Life

In everyday life telepathy can be found in many places: as conscious telepathy, when one searches for something or calls someone inwardly – then the more inconspicuous telepathy with intuition and empathy or when being stared at – the "magic wish", which is fulfilled after a short time – the taking of a homeopathic remedy – being pushed into a role by a dominant person …

The variety is great and in most places where telepathy occurs, it is hardly noticed.

If the previous descriptions in this book are true, there is a complex network of telepathic connections between all living beings and also between them and the Earth itself. This "telepathic network" coordinates all events in such a way that they remain in harmony with each other – how else could astrology describe the character of a person in a striking and detailed way and, moreover, predict events? This "telepathic network" may also be called "collective subconsciousness".

Thus, telepathy is not something that is possible only for particularly gifted people, but it is a small thread in a big whole that coordinates all events with each other. Everyone can become aware of these "telepathic threads" and then use them consciously. This can be experienced as "intentional telepathy".

10. Learning Telepathy

Now at the end of this book the question arises, how one can learn telepathy. For the answer to this question it is of central importance that one does not have to "make" telepathy first, but that the telepathic connections between all beings already exist – in homeopathy, in astrology, in telepathy, in wishing, in magic …

This means that it is not a question of creating something with a lot of force and effort, but instead to look with attention to what is already there. In learning telepathy, listening helps more than effort: Meditating, being able to become quiet inside, being in the here and now, doing dream journeys, talking to one's own organs, listening to one's own intuition …

Of course, it also helps to experiment a bit – alone or with friends. Many experiments are very simple and have a great effect – like the postcard experiment and the paper wheel experiment. Once you have experienced telepathy, telekinesis, astrology, etc. a few times, and have been able to help yourself with an illness, for example, by dream traveling to the sick organ, you will realize not only the reality, but also the great benefits of telepathy in everyday life.

There is not the one best telepathy exercise that will make you a "telepathy master" in three months … learning telepathy is always also getting to know yourself, because telepathy takes place in the subconsciousness (astral body). Everything that leads to one's own center also promotes telepathy and telekinesis, since learning these two things is primarily about the waking consciousness being able to specifically perceive the contents of the subconsciousness.

However, striving to live from one's own center does not necessarily immediately lead to telepathic phenomena as well – sooner or later, however, these abilities will arise, but not necessarily immediately. In yoga, these abilities are called "siddhis" and are viewed rather suspiciously because they might distract the yogi from his meditation.

However, when viewed more from a magician's point of view, these abilities are desirable – but they can only be attained to a limited extent as long as one does not heal one's inner self, otherwise old wounds and feelings will hinder the contact between the waking consciousness and the subconsciousness.

From the point of view of a yogi, such abilities as telepathy and telekinesis are actually rather things that interfere with meditation – from the point of view of the magician, they are what he wants to achieve. The yogi therefore pays no attention to these abilities, while the magician concentrates on them and explores them with the help of experiments.

Now, one does not have to adopt either of these extreme attitudes, but can strive for one's own center, and at the same time make a few experiments in order to fathom the possibilities of man in this world. Thereby one will become more faithful to oneself

as well as expand one's own possibilities of action.
  Probably this is the most effective approach to live happily.

English Books by Harry Eilenstein	
- Living Magic (261 p.)	- Meditation for Beginners
- The Synthesis of Physics and Magic (192 p.)	- Kundalini for Beginners
- Telepathy for Beginners (60 p.)	- Chakra-Magic for Beginners
- Astral Projection for Beginners (60 p.)	- Astrology for Beginners
- Invocations for Beginners (52 p.)	- Ritual Magic for Beginners
- Evocations for Beginners (62 p.)	- Mandalas for Beginners
- Auto-Movement for Beginners (60 p.)	- Love Magic for Beginners
- Elves for Beginners (56 p.)	- Magic Research for Beginners
- Hypnosis for Beginners (56 p.)	- Self-awareness for Beginners
- Money Magic for Beginners (60 p.)	- Symbolism of Numbers for Beginners
- Magic Objects for Beginners (64 p.)	- Language of the Moon – for Beginners
- Shamanism for Beginners (52 p.)	- Magic Chant for Beginners
- Crop Circles for Beginners (344 p.)	- Prophecy for Beginners
- Number Symbolism for Beginners (64 p.)	- Da'ath-Magic for Beginners
	- Feng Shui for Beginners
These books will be puplished soon:	- Magic for Beginners – Anthology I
- Telepathy for Advanced Learners	- Magic for Beginners – Anthology II
- Telekinesis for Beginners	- Magic for Beginners – Anthology III
- Life Force for Beginners	- Magic for Beginners – Anthology IV

Bücher von Harry Eilenstein	
Religion allgemein	**Germanen**
- Die sieben Schritte des Lebens (428 S.)	- Die Götter der Germanen (87 Bände – siehe nächste Seite)
- Muttergöttin und Schamanen (168 S.)	- Odin (300 S.)
- Göbekli Tepe (472 S.)	**Kelten**
- Die Göttin von Göbekli Tepe (144 S.)	- Cernunnos (690 S.)
- Totempfähle (440 S.)	- Taliesin (228 S.)
- Christus (60 S.)	- Der Kessel von Gundestrup (220 S.)
- Dakini (80 S.)	- Der Chiemsee-Kessel (76)
- Vajra (76 S.)	**Psychologie**
Ägypten	- Über die Freude (100 S.)
- Hathor und Re 1: Götter und Mythen im Alten Ägypten (432 S.)	- Das Geheimnis des inneren Friedens (252 S.)
- Hathor und Re 2: Die altägyptische Religion – Ursprünge, Kult und Magie (396 S.)	- Das Beziehungsmandala (52 S.)
	- Gefühle und ihre Verwandlungen (404 S.)
- Isis (508 S.)	- einsgerichtet (140 S.)
Indogermanen	- Liebe und Eigenständigkeit (216 S.)
- Die Entwicklung der indogermanischen Religionen (700 S.)	- Von innerer Fülle zu äußerem Gedeihen (52 S.)
	Heilung
- Wurzeln und Zweige der indogermanischen Religion (224 S.)	- Die Symbolik der Krankheiten (76 S.)
	Kunst
	- Herz des Tanzes – Tanz des Herzens (160 S.)
	Drama
	- König Athelstan (104 S.)

Bücher von Harry Eilenstein

„Magie für Anfänger"
- Telepathie für Anfänger (60 S.)
- Telepathie für Fortgeschrittene (52 S.)
- Telekinese für Anfänger (52 S.)
- Lebenskraft für Anfänger (60 S.)
- Meditation für Anfänger (56 S.)
- Kundalini für Anfänger (100 S.)
- Hypnose für Anfänger (56 S.)
- Auto-Movement für Anfänger (56 S.)
- Chakra-Magie für Anfänger (148 S.)
- Astralreisen für Anfänger (56 S.)
- Astrologie für Anfänger (120 S.)
- Ritual-Magie für Anfänger (56 S.)
- Mandalas für Anfänger (68 S.)
- Geldzauber für Anfänger (56 S.)
- Liebeszauber für Anfänger (52 S.)
- Invokationen für Anfänger (52 S.)
- Evokationen für Anfänger (60 S.)
- Elfen für Anfänger (56 S.)
- Magie-Forschung für Anfänger (140 S.)
- Selbsterkenntnis für Anfänger (52 S.)
- Zahlensymbolik für Anfänger (60 S.)
- Die Sprache des Mondes – für Anfänger (116 S.)
- Zaubergesänge für Anfänger (100 S.)
- Zukunftschau für Anfänger (60 S.)
- Schamanismus für Anfänger (52 S.)
- Magische Gegenstände für Anfänger (68 S.)
- Da'ath-Magie für Anfänger (64 S.)
- Kornkreise für Anfänger (348 S.)
- Feng Shui für Anfänger (96 S.)
- Magie für Anfänger – Sammelband I (696 S.)
- Magie für Anfänger – Sammelband II (664 S.)
- Magie für Anfänger – Sammelband III (580 S.)

„Traumreisen"
- Traumreisen zu Heilpflanzen (700 S.)

Magie
- Handbuch für Zauberlehrlinge (408 S.)
- Tarot (104 S.)
- Physik und Magie (184 S.)
- Die Synthese von Physik und Magie (200S.)
- Die Magie-Formel (156 S.)
- Krafttiere – Tiergöttinnen – Tiertänze (112 S.)
- Schwitzhütten (524 S.)
- Mythen und Magie der Harfe (116 S.)
- Magie heute – Berichte aus der Praxis (288 S.)

Meditation
- Der Lebenskraftkörper (230 S.)
- Die Chakren (100 S.)
- Das Chakren-System mit den Nebenchakren (296 S.)
- Organe und Chakren (64 S.)
- Die platonischen Körper in den Chakren (156 S.)
- Meditation (140 S.)
- Drachenfeuer (124 S.)
- Kundalini I (676 S.)
- Reinkarnation (156 S.)
- einsgerichtet (140 S.)

Astrologie
- Astrologie (496 S.)
- Photo-Astrologie (428 S.)
- Die astrologischen Aspekte (88 S.)
- Horoskop und Seele (120 S.)

Kabbala
- Kursus der praktischen Kabbala (150 S.)
- Eltern der Erde (450 S.)
- Blüten des Lebensbaumes:
    - Die Struktur des kabbalistischen Lebensbaumes (370 S.)
    - Der kabbalistische Lebensbaum als Forschungshilfsmittel (580 S.)
    - Der kabbalistische Lebensbaum als spirituelle Landkarte (520 S.)

Die Themen der 87 Bände der Reihe „Die Götter der Germanen"

1. Die Entwicklung der germanischen Religion
2. Lexikon der germanischen Religion
3. Der ursprüngliche Göttervater Tyr
4. Tyr in der Unterwelt: der Schmied Wieland
5. Tyr in der Unterwelt: der Riesenkönig Teil 1
6. Tyr in der Unterwelt: der Riesenkönig Teil 2
7. Tyr in der Unterwelt: der Zwergenkönig
8. Der Himmelswächter Heimdall
9. Der Sommergott Baldur
10. Der Meeresgott: Ägir, Hler und Njörd
11. Der Eibengott Ullr
12. Die Zwillingsgötter Alcis
13. Der neue Göttervater Odin Teil 1
14. Der neue Göttervater Odin Teil 2
15. Der Fruchtbarkeitsgott Freyr
16. Der Chaos-Gott Loki
17. Der Donnergott Thor
18. Der Priestergott Hönir
19. Die Göttersöhne
20. Die unbekannteren Götter
21. Die Göttermutter Frigg
22. Die Liebesgöttin: Freya und Menglöd
23. Die Erdgöttinnen
24. Die Korngöttin Sif
25. Die Apfel-Göttin Idun
26. Die Hügelgrab-Jenseitsgöttin Hel
27. Die Meeres-Jenseitsgöttin Ran
28. Die unbekannteren Jenseitsgöttinnen
29. Die unbekannteren Göttinnen
30. Die Nornen
31. Die Walküren
32. Die Zwerge
33. Der Urriese Ymir
34. Die Riesen
35. Die Riesinnen
36. Mythologische Wesen
37. Mythologische Priester und Priesterinnen
38. Sigurd/Siegfried
39. Helden und Göttersöhne
40. Die Symbolik der Vögel und Insekten
41. Die Symbolik der Schlangen, Drachen und Ungeheuer
42.a Die Symbolik der Herdentiere I
42.b Die Symbolik der Herdentiere II
43. Die Symbolik der Raubtiere
44. Die Symbolik der Wassertiere und sonstigen Tiere
45. Die Symbolik der Pflanzen
46. Die Symbolik der Farben
47. Die Symbolik der Zahlen
48. Die Symbolik von Sonne, Mond und Sternen
49.a Das Jenseits I – Das Hügelgrab
49.b Das Jenseits II – Der Jenseitsweg
50. Seelenvogel, Utiseta und Einweihung
51. Wiederzeugung und Wiedergeburt
52. Elemente der Kosmologie
53. Der Weltenbaum
54. Die Symbolik der Himmelsrichtungen und der Jahreszeiten
55.a Mythologische Motive I
55.b Mythologische Motive II
56. Der Tempel
57. Die Einrichtung des Tempels
58. Priesterin – Seherin – Zauberin – Hexe
59. Priester – Seher – Zauberer
60. Rituelle Kleidung und Schmuck
61. Skalden und Skaldinnen
62 Kriegerinnen und Ekstase-Krieger
63. Die Symbolik der Körperteile
64.a Magie und Ritual I
64.b Magie und Ritual II
64.c Magie und Ritual III
65. Gestaltwandlungen
66.a Magische Angriffs-Waffen
66.b Magische Verteidigungs-Waffen
67. Magische Werkzeuge und Gegenstände
68. Zaubersprüche
69. Göttermet
70. Zaubertränke
71. Träume, Omen und Orakel
72. Runen
73. Sozial-religiöse Rituale
74. Weisheiten und Sprichworte
75. Kenningar
76. Rätsel
77. Die vollständige Edda des Snorri Sturluson
78. Frühe Skaldenlieder
79.a Mythologische Sagas I
79.b Mythologische Sagas II
80. Hymnen an die germanischen Götter